It was hot. The sun was shining and the Mrs Cherry's parrot.
"What a day for a bike ride!" said Sam.
He raced down to get Info-rider. It was leaning against the wall, gleaming in the sunlight.

Sam pulled on his helmet and jumped onto Info-rider.
"Where to, Sam?" the screen flashed.
"Kim's place," said Sam.

Mum came out.

"Where are you off to?" she asked.

"Kim's place," said Sam.

"That's nice. Bring Kim back for tea if you like," said Mum.

"Thanks, Mum. Bye, Grandad!" Sam called as he raced off.

Sam sped past Mrs Cherry's garden.
"Where are you going?" she asked.
"Kim's place – can't stop!" Sam yelled.
"Have fun, dear!" said Mrs Cherry.
"Fun, dear! Fun, dear!" squawked Blue.

Two seconds later Sam was outside Kim's house.
The screen flashed, "Kim's not at home."
"I bet she's on the hill," said Sam. "Let's go!"

"Faster! Faster!" yelled Sam as he raced towards the hill.
He skidded round the bend and onto the hill.
"Nice one, Sam," flashed the screen.

"Over the bridge?" asked Info-rider.
"You bet!" said Sam, and rode towards the bridge.
Suddenly the screen flashed, "Look out!"
Then a voice shouted, "Stop!"

Sam braked hard and skidded to a stop. Kev was standing in front of the bridge. He was barring the way.
"This is my bridge now!" shouted Kev. "You can't cross it."
"It isn't your bridge and I can cross it if I want to," said Sam.

"I might let you cross it – but only if you let me have a go on your bike," said Kev.
"No way!" yelled Sam, and he held on tightly to Info-rider.
"A bike like this is too good for a kid like you!" said Kev. He grabbed the front wheel.

Sam held on tightly. He glared at Kev. Kev glared at Sam. Sam was no baby but Kev was big… very big.
"Push off, kid!" yelled Kev. "Info-rider's all mine now."
"Don't bet on it," said Sam.

Then Sam shouted at the top of his voice, "Go, Info-rider!" At once Info-rider broke away from Kev and took off like a rocket.
"Jump!" shouted Sam. "Jump!"
"Hold on!" flashed the screen.

Sam jumped up, up high, right over Kev's head.
"Nice one, Info-rider!" yelled Sam.
He landed smoothly on the bridge and raced off.
"Wow!" said Kev. "What a bike! I've got to get my hands on it."

Sam rode towards the hut. Kim was there, whizzing around on her skates.

"Hi, Kim!" said Sam.

"Hi, Sam," said Kim. "Did you see Kev at the bridge? He tried to stop me crossing it. I had to skate around him."

"That big bully!" said Sam. "He tried to get my bike, too. I jumped right over his head!"

Kim grinned. "I wish I'd seen that! Come on, I'll race you. Give me a head start."

"You're on!"

Sam and Kim shot off like rockets. They raced up and down and round and round. First Sam beat Kim. Then Kim beat Sam.
"Who's the winner?" asked Kim at last.
"Let's call it a draw!" said Sam.

They sat down on the grass to rest.
"Can I have a go on your bike, Sam?" asked Kim.
"Yes, if I can have a go on your skates," said Sam.
"OK," said Kim, "but they might be a bit small for you."

Sam started to take off his trainers. As he was putting on Kim's skates, he heard something. He looked round just in time to see Kev racing off on Info-rider.
"Hey!" yelled Sam. "That's my bike!"
"You can't catch me!" shouted Kev. "I've got the fastest bike in Hops Hill!"

"Not for long," said Sam.
He tried to race after Kev, but Kim's skates were too small for him to skate fast.
"What shall I do?" he said. "I must think of a plan."
He watched Kev racing along, going faster and faster.

"Got it!" said Sam.

He took a deep, deep breath and shouted at the top of his voice, "Info-rider! Stop! Stop now!"

At once Info-rider braked hard. Kev nearly fell off.

"Hey!" Kev screamed. "What's happening? Hey!"
He pushed on the pedals but they wouldn't move. He tried to turn the bike around but it wouldn't move.
Then Sam shouted, "Info-rider! Come back here!"
At once the bike started going backwards very fast.

"Help! Stop! Help!" shrieked Kev as the bike raced backwards.
"Info-rider – jump! Turn! Spin!" shouted Sam.
The bike jumped, turned and spun round and round. Kev's face was very green.
"St-stop! Make it stop!" he screamed as he whizzed around at top speed.

"Well, OK," said Sam. "Info-rider – stop!"
At once the bike screeched to a stop. Kev shot off the bike and landed on the ground with a thump.
"Ouch!" he groaned.
"Do you give up?" asked Sam.
"Keep your rotten bike," shrieked Kev. "I don't want it anyway!"

"Ha!" said Kim. "That showed him!"

"Thanks to Info-rider," said Sam. He skated over to Info-rider and picked it up. "What a bike!"

"Yes, what a bike!" said Kim. "Can I have a go now?"

"OK!" said Sam with a big grin.

"Race you back to my place for tea!" he said.
"OK! I'll give you a head start," said Kim.
They both raced off. Sam was on Kim's skates. Kim was on Info-rider. Kim won!